AF430668

RED

SQUARE

YELLOW

CIRCLE

PINK

RECTANGLE

GREEN

TRIANGLE

PURPLE

OVAL

ORANGE

PENTAGON

BLUE

HEXAGON

RED

CROSS

YELLOW

OCTAGON

PINK

PARALLELOGRAM

GREEN

TRAPEZOID

PURPLE

ARROW

ORANGE

STAR

BLUE

HEART

RED

CUBE

YELLOW

NONAGON

PINK

DECAGON

GREEN

CYLINDER

PURPLE

SEMI CIRCLE

ORANGE

CONE

BLUE

CUBOID

#SHAPES
&
#COLOURS

18 DIFFERENT SHAPES FOR YOU TO REMEMBER

BRAIN POWER

Thank you!